UNODA

United Nations Office for
Disarmament Affairs

I0117037

CIVIL SOCIETY AND DISARMAMENT 2015

Statements of Non-Governmental Organizations at the 2015 Review Conference of the Parties to the Treaty on the Non-Proliferation of Nuclear Weapons

United Nations

Note

The United Nations Office for Disarmament Affairs is publishing this material within the context of General Assembly resolution 69/71 on the United Nations Disarmament Information Programme in order to further an informed debate on topical issues of arms limitation, disarmament and security.

This publication contains the statements made by representatives of non-governmental organizations on 1 May 2015 during the 2015 Review Conference of the Parties to the Treaty on the Non-Proliferation of Nuclear Weapons, held at the United Nations, New York. The material appearing in this book is in unedited and original form as submitted by the authors. The views of the authors do not necessarily reflect those of the United Nations or its Member States.

Symbols of United Nations documents are composed of capital letters combined with figures. These documents are available in the official languages of the United Nations at http://ods.un.org. Specific disarmament-related documents can also be accessed through the disarmament reference collection at http://www.un.org/disarmament/HomePage/library.shtml.

This publication is available at

www.un.org/disarmament

UNITED NATIONS PUBLICATION
Sales No. E.16.IX.3

ISBN 978-92-1-142309-9
eISBN 978-92-1-057805-9

Contents

Foreword

Five years after the adoption of the nuclear Non-Proliferation Treaty (NPT) Action Plan in 2010, states parties of the Treaty met to review its implementation. Compliance with commitments related to nuclear disarmament lagged far behind those related to non-proliferation or the peaceful uses of nuclear energy, and states possessing nuclear weapons were found to be continuing to invest in their arsenals. Tensions among nuclear-armed states were raised, and in the end, the Review Conference was unable to adopt an outcome because Israel, a non-state party, did not agree to its terms.

This state of play lies at the centre of the critique of many of the civil society presentations to the 2015 NPT Review Conference. The statements contained in this publication indicate an overwhelming sense of frustration at the injustice of a handful of states continuing to possess and modernise nuclear weapons while the rest of the world is told that conditions are not yet right for disarmament.

However, non-nuclear-armed states and civil society have not been idle since 2010. That Review Conference expressed "deep concern at the catastrophic humanitarian consequences of any use of nuclear weapons." Since then, especially at the series of conferences hosted by Norway, Mexico, and Austria, these consequences have increasingly become a focal point for discussion and proposed action. Governments are also increasingly raising the issue of humanitarian impacts in traditional forums, with 159 states signing a joint statement at the 2015 Review Conference highlighting the unacceptable harm caused by nuclear weapons and calling for action to ensure they are never used again, under any circumstances.

The humanitarian initiative has provided the basis for a new momentum on nuclear disarmament. It has involved new types of actors, such as the Red Cross and Red Crescent Movement, the United Nations Office for Coordination of Humanitarian Affairs, and a new generation of civil society campaigners. The humanitarian initiative has also resulted in the Humanitarian Pledge, which commits its endorsers to "fill the legal gap for the prohibition and elimination of nuclear weapons." As of December 2015, 121 states have endorsed the Pledge. These states are committed to change. They believe that existing international law is inadequate for achieving nuclear disarmament and that a process of change that involves stigmatising, prohibiting, and eliminating nuclear weapons is necessary.

As several of the civil society presentations in this publication argue, this process requires a legally-binding international instrument that clearly prohibits nuclear weapons based on their unacceptable consequences. Such a treaty would put nuclear weapons on the same footing as the other weapons of mass destruction, which are subject to prohibition through specific treaties. A treaty banning nuclear weapons would build on existing norms and reinforce existing legal instruments, including the NPT, but it would also close loopholes in the current legal regime that enable states to engage in nuclear weapon activities or to otherwise claim perceived benefit from the continued existence of nuclear weapons while purporting to promote their elimination.

It is past time that the NPT nuclear-armed states and their nuclear-dependent allies fulfill their responsibilities, commitments, and obligations—or risk undermine the very treaty regime they claim to want to protect. Their failure to implement their commitments presents dim prospects for the future of the NPT. The apparent expectation that this non-compliance can continue in perpetuity, allowing not only for continued possession but also modernisation and deployment of nuclear weapon systems, is misguided.

NPT states parties need to ask themselves how long we can wait for disarmament. Several initiatives since the 2010 Review Conference have advanced the ongoing international discussion about nuclear weapons. States and other actors must now be willing to act to achieve disarmament, by developing a legally-binding instrument to prohibit and establish a framework for eliminating nuclear weapons. We are at the end of the year of the 70th anniversary of the US atomic bombings of Hiroshima and Nagasaki. It is past time for action.

Ray **Acheson**
Director, Reaching Critical Will
NGO coordinator of the
2015 NPT Review Conference

Statement by the Arms Control Association
Speaker: Daryl Kimball

Greater United States and Russian cooperation and leadership is necessary to fulfil NPT Article VI obligations to reduce and eliminate nuclear dangers

Since the inception of the NPT, the United States and Russia—the world's first nuclear-weapon States and still the possessors of the largest and most deadly nuclear arsenals—have been central to the success or the failure of the treaty.

Through the decades, U.S.-Russian bilateral nuclear disarmament treaties have slowly, but significantly reduced the arsenals of the Cold War years, reduced tensions, and lowered the threat of a nuclear exchange.

Despite that progress, today Russia possesses some 1,780 nuclear warheads and the United States some 1,900 thermonuclear warheads[1] that can be delivered on several hundred strategic bombers and missiles—far more than necessary to deter nuclear attack. (Thousands more warheads are held in reserve or awaiting dismantlement.) If these weapons were used even in a "limited" way, the result would be catastrophic global nuclear devastation.

U.S. and Russian nuclear strategy still requires a launch-on-warning or launch-under-attack capability, which "puts an enormous strain on the nuclear chains of command in both countries" and

---

[1] According to research from Hans Kristensen and Stan Norris published in the *Bulletin of the Atomic Scientists* this year. The U.S. and Russia currently deploy just under 1,600 New START-accountable strategic warheads. Under New START, bombers are counted as one weapon each because the bomber weapons are not loaded on bombers. When bomber weapons at bomber bases are counted, the number of strategic nuclear weapons available for potential use is much higher.

perpetuates the risk of cataclysmic error according to retired senior U.S. and Russian generals.[2]

In 2008, President-elect Barack Obama said: "Keeping nuclear weapons ready to launch on a moment's notice is a dangerous relic of the Cold War. Such policies increase the risk of catastrophic accidents or miscalculation. I believe that we must address this dangerous situation—something that President Bush promised to do when he campaigned for president back in 2000, but did not do once in office. I will work with Russia to end such outdated Cold War policies in a mutual and verifiable way."[3]

U.S.-Russian leadership on nuclear disarmament and arms control is still essential to avoiding catastrophe and ensuring that the Nuclear Nonproliferation Treaty regime remains strong and viable.

Following the conclusion of the 2010 New Strategic Arms Reduction accord, Moscow and Washington have failed to start talks to further reduce their still enormous nuclear stockpiles, which still far exceed any plausible deterrence requirements. Despite adjustments to its missile defense plans in Europe that eliminate any threat to Russian strategic missiles, Russian President Vladimir Putin rebuffed U.S. President Obama's June 2013 proposal to reduce U.S. and Russian strategic nuclear stockpiles by one-third below the ceilings set by New START.

Then, last year, Russia interfered with the territorial integrity of Ukraine and annexed Crimea in flagrant disregard of the great powers' pledge to respect Ukrainian sovereignty following Kiev's decision in 1994 to join the NPT as a nonnuclear weapon state.

Since then, Russian relations with the United States and Europe have hit their lowest point in more than a quarter century. New negotiations on further nuclear disarmament beyond New START are unlikely any time soon, and both sides are considering new options for countering the conventional and nuclear capabilities of the other side.

---

[2] See: "How to Avert a Nuclear War," by James E. Cartwright and Vladimir Dvorkin, *The New York Times*, April 19, 2015.

[3] "2008 Presidential Q & A: President-elect Barack Obama," *Arms Control Today*, December 2008.

For now, the two sides continue to respect and implement the 2010 New START Treaty. But neither the United States nor Russia is meeting their 2010 NPT Review Conference pledge to accelerate and deepen the verifiable reduction of their nuclear stockpiles.

Meanwhile, NATO has, for several years now, been unable to agree on a proposal for transparency and accounting for Russian and U.S. tactical nuclear weapons. Russia, for its part, refuses to engage in talks on tactical nuclear weapons. As a result, neither side is meeting their 2010 NPT pledge to pursue talks on sub-strategic nuclear weapons.

In addition, there are allegations that Russia tested a new ground-launched cruise missile prohibited under the 1987 Intermediate-Range Nuclear Forces (INF) Treaty. Russia has made countercharges about U.S. violations. U.S. and Russian officials say they are interested in discussing the issue, but the matter remains unresolved.

Neither Russia nor the United States says they want to scrap the existing arms control regime, including New START and the INF Treaty, which provide greater predictability and stability in an otherwise strained bilateral relationship. But if tensions worsen further, these treaties could be in trouble.

Scrapping the existing nuclear risk reduction measures would do nothing to protect Ukraine from further Russian aggression or reassure nervous NATO members, nor would it enhance Russia's security.

At the same time, Moscow and Washington are busy modernizing their nuclear weapons and delivery systems, as are France and the United Kingdom. China is continuing to modernize and expand its nuclear forces. These actions are inconsistent with their Article VI NPT commitments. Meanwhile, a technological nuclear arms race between India and Pakistan is also underway.

Statements by officials from NPT nuclear weapon states threatening the use of nuclear weapons—directly or indirectly— are also inconsistent with the aims and purpose of the NPT. Such statements, including vague "all options are on the table" statements, are often intended to intimidate or coerce other states. Such threats are counterproductive and undermine international peace and stability.

The mere possession of nuclear weapons is a sufficient reminder they may be used.

+ + +

This review conference and the key states with nuclear weapons must recognize that the world is on the cusp of unconstrained strategic nuclear competition, which would not only deepen the distrust and increase dangers, but also would undermine the NPT.

States parties must also recognize that, despite the modest progress achieved through New START, the threat of nuclear war between the major nuclear powers is still with us and would have catastrophic global impacts.

This conference cannot afford to paper over these cold realities with bland statements and restatements of past pledges or, as the U.S. government does, by citing how many nuclear weapons have been reduced since 1970.

As President Obama correctly noted in a speech in 2012, "[t]he massive nuclear arsenal we inherited from the Cold War is poorly suited for today's threats," and "we have more nuclear weapons than we need."

Creative, practical ideas are needed to overcome old obstacles and excuses. We urge all states at this conference and all NGOs to come together around four major sets of actions to help reduce nuclear dangers and fulfill the promise of the NPT:

1.   *Accelerate U.S.-Russian New START Implementation*

In 2010, all of the nuclear-weapon states committed "to accelerate concrete progress on the steps leading to nuclear disarmament," including "all types of nuclear weapons."

Further nuclear reductions need not wait for a new U.S.-Russian arms control treaty. The final document for this Conference should call upon the United States and Russia to accelerate the pace of reductions under New START to reach the agreed limits before the 2018 deadline and call on both states to continue to reduce force levels below the New START ceilings, to be verified with the treaty's monitoring regime.

2. Initiate New START Follow-On Talks No Later Than 2017

This Conference should also call upon the leaders in Moscow and Washington to begin formal negotiations on a follow-on to the New START accord no later than 2017.

Many U.S., Russian, and European experts recommend that such a follow-on agreement should aim to cut each side's strategic arsenals to fewer than 1,100 deployed strategic warheads and 500 deployed strategic delivery vehicles, including any strategic-range conventional prompt-strike weapons. Such talks can and should explore a wider range of issues, including transparency and confidence-building steps on tactical nuclear weapons and joint understandings on missile defense capabilities and deployments.[4]

3. Reinforce the INF Treaty and Discuss Global Nuclear-Armed Cruise Missile Limits

To reinforce and expand the INF Treaty, this Conference should underscore the value of the INF Treaty, which commits the parties not to test, produce, or deploy ground-launched missile systems with ranges between 500 and 5,500 kilometers, and call upon the United States and Russia to agree to special measures, perhaps including inspections, to resolve compliance concerns.

Russia and the United States should also be invited to engage with other states in talks on limiting and eventually phasing out all nuclear-armed cruise missile systems. This would allow the two countries to forgo expensive modernization programs for such missiles, and in cooperation with other key states, head off dangerous cruise missile buildups around the globe.

4. Call On Other Nuclear-Armed States to Freeze Their Nuclear Build-ups

This Conference must recognize that the world's other nuclear-armed states must do their part to advance Article VI goals too.

---

[4] "Second Report of the Deep Cuts Commission: Strengthening Stability in Turbulent Times," published by the Institute for Peace Research and Security Policy at the University of Hamburg, April 2015. Online at: www.deepcuts.org.

In addition to urging the United States, China, and the other CTBT Annex II states to finally take the steps necessary to ratify the Comprehensive Nuclear-Test-Ban Treaty, China and the world's other nuclear-armed states should be called upon by all NPT states parties to freeze the overall size of their stockpiles as long as the United States and Russia continue to reduce their nuclear arsenals.

A unified push for further U.S.-Russian arms cuts combined with a global nuclear weapons freeze by the other nuclear-armed states would help create the conditions for multilateral, verifiable nuclear disarmament and an eventual ban on nuclear weapons.

5.   Examine dangerous doctrines

In 2010, all of the NPT nuclear-weapon states committed to "diminish the role and significance of nuclear weapons" and "[d]iscuss policies that could prevent the use of nuclear weapons." Unfortunately, few have undertaken demonstrable, concrete steps to do so.

The final document for this NPT Review Conference should require each of the world's nuclear-armed states to report, in detail and before the first preparatory committee meeting for the 2020 Review Conference, the physical, environmental, and human impacts of their nuclear war plans, if these plans were to be carried out, and how they believe the use of hundreds of such weapons would be consistent with humanitarian law and the laws of war as some nuclear-armed states claim.[5]

Given the catastrophic consequences of the large-scale use of nuclear weapons against many dozens—if not hundreds—of targets, as envisioned in the U.S., Russian, French, Chinese, British, Indian and Pakistani nuclear war plans, it is hard to see how the use of significant numbers of nuclear weapons could be consistent with

---

[5] The June 2013 Report on the Nuclear Weapons Employment Strategy of the United States claims that: "[t]he new guidance makes clear that all plans must be consistent with the fundamental principles of the Law of Armed Conflict. Accordingly, plans will, for example, apply the principles of distinction and proportionality and seek to minimize collateral damage to civilian populations and civilian objects. The United States will not intentionally target civilian populations or civilian objects."

international humanitarian law or any common sense interpretation of the Law of Armed Conflict.

To reduce the risk of inadvertent nuclear weapons use, the presidents of Russia and the United States should, as retired Generals Cartwright and Dvorkin have recommended, "decide in tandem to eliminate the launch on warning concept from their nuclear strategies." This would not undermine "strategic stability" since both countries have nuclear forces designed to withstand an initial first-strike. The Conference should also call upon all nuclear-armed states to pursue a legally- or politically-binding agreement to refrain from putting their nuclear weapons on high alert, as suggested by the Global Zero Commission on Nuclear Risk Reduction.[6]

The NPT nuclear-weapon states should be required to report to fellow NPT states parties on specific changes to their targeting and nuclear weapons employment doctrines that reduce the role of nuclear weapons and reduce the risk that their nuclear weapons may be used deliberately or accidentally.

Today, as during the Cold War, effective, persistent nuclear arms control leadership is in the best interests of Russia, the United States, and the world.

In the coming months and years, creative, bold approaches will be needed to overcome old and new obstacles to the long-running effort to eliminate the potential for nuclear catastrophe.

Endorsed by:

Derek Johnson, Executive Director, Global Zero

Daryl Kimball, Executive Director, Arms Control Association

Ulrich Kühn, Executive of the trilateral Commission on Challenges Deep Nuclear Cuts*

Paul Meyer, Fellow in International Security, Simon Fraser University and Senior Fellow, The Simons Foundation

---

[6] *De-Alerting and Stabilizing the World's Nuclear Force Postures*, Global Zero Commission on Nuclear Risk Reduction, April 2015.

* Institution listed for identification purposes only.

Götz Neuneck, Deputy Director Institute for Peace Research and Security Policy at the University of Hamburg

Steve Pifer, Senior Fellow, the Brookings Institution*

Greg Thielmann, Senior Fellow, Arms Control Association

Paul Walker, Director, Environmental Security and Sustainability, Green Cross International

Lisbeth Gronlund and David Wright, Co-Directors, Global Security Program, Union of Concerned Scientists

---

* Institution listed for identification purposes only.

Statement by Ban All Nukes generation
Speakers: Josie Parkhouse and Sampson Oppedisano

Madam President and Delegates,

Today, we stand before you as idealistic youth. We are not ashamed of this fact. We stand here because we believe the statements of the Nuclear Weapon States do not represent the majority of young people within their borders. We're here to speak on behalf of these young people and we believe that a better world can be created: a world without nuclear weapons. I'm sure everyone in this room today can remember being young and having dreams of making the world a better place. The United Nations is built on this ideal. But some, who are present, have forgotten this idealism; you've lost your way along the path.

We ask you all to take a moment today to remember why you went into world affairs, remember the idealism of your youth and return to your former aspirational path. Unless we preserve the daring energy to look beyond the reality of today to a vision of a better tomorrow, we will continue to face the walls of apathy and defeatism. To stay on our current path is to give into fear and accept a less than safe world.

Madam President,

A nuclear attack would be devastating and as Secretary General Ban-Ki-Moon reminded us, we only have to listen to the accounts of the victims of nuclear weapon use and testing to understand how no country could adequately respond. Unfortunately, keeping our heads in the sand is to continue to trust those that tell us that nuclear weapons keep us safe, that they will never be used again, and that they are a deterrent for other countries. Perhaps these convenient, unreflective and uncritical arguments veered you off the path of peace in the first place. After all, we are often told that because there has been no nuclear war for the last 70 years, we can assume that this will continue for the rest of history.

This illogical attitude can be summed up well by an analogy of a man falling from a skyscraper. Those half-way up the building heard him shout as he passed their window, "So far so good." We're often told as NGOs we are unrealistic in fighting for a nuclear weapon free world, but in fact basing world security on the "so far, so good" recipe, we see that it is the nuclear weapon states that are being unrealistic. Clearly, "so far so good" is not a recipe for world security. The worst is possible.

Madam President,

We live in a highly interdependent world where the actions of one can effect us all. Even if we choose only to seek our own national interest, in today's globalized world, this cannot be achieved without cooperating beyond our borders. All of our actions have an effect and this conference can either go down in history as just another review conference, or it can down in history as *the* review conference which led to a ban on nuclear weapons.

However to achieve this requires real action, not just empty words and promises. Action based on the shared trust and respect for our world, for each other, for the environment and for humanity.

Just as this conference can affect the whole of humanity, nuclear weapons used by anyone will have an immediate effect on everyone. Let's take a long term view and by doing so, realize the importance of acting in this moment, at this conference.

Madam President,

Today we find ourselves defending our peace and security more frequently from unpredictable threats. Be it the outbreak of Ebola or the rise of terrorist groups such as ISIS, our commitment to achieving lasting peace and security is increasingly tested.

And yet, despite constantly reaffirming this commitment to pursuing a more safe and peaceful world, many leaders continue to ignore a threat that is within our power to end.

To the nuclear weapons states we ask, what contributions to global peace and security are your nuclear stockpiles making? Your continued investment and modernization of such useless weapons is not only a threat to all, but divests valuable resources away from services in education, healthcare, and development—prerequisites for the secure world you all claim to strive for.

Quite frankly it's ironic that we've reached a point where the youth at this conference are acting more responsibly in regards to disarmament than many of the adults charged with handling the task in the first place.

Your inability to take action is appalling and resembles that of a child who procrastinates their homework until the last minute. The big difference here is that waiting until the last minute won't lead to a bad report card, but rather to the potential destruction of humanity.

You see it's simple; a world where nuclear weapons exist is not a secure world. It is not a world where peace and trust between nations can begin to grow, and it is not a world that, we the youth, plan to inherit.

Madam President,

Today, we find ourselves at a crossroad, and the path we choose *will* decide our future.

The first path leads us to a future where continued empty promises only prevent progress from being made. To continue down this path is to give into fear; a groundless fear that nuclear deterrence is the only means to a secure and peaceful world.

However, the second path is one many of you have fallen off of. This path leads us back to the idealism and pragmatic energy needed for a better tomorrow. Here we confront our fears through diplomacy and understanding and once again pursue the future we all deserve.

In closing, Madam President and Delegates,

During a time where tensions amongst nations are on the rise, we understand that the task before us is not an easy one. But know this:

A star shines brightest when surrounded by darkness. It is during our most trying times that we've proven that we can rise to the occasion.

We the youth are ready to do our part. The question is, are you all? Will you all continue down the path of fear, Or, will you all remember why you've dedicated your lives to making the world a better place, and return to the path of idealism.

A wise person is one who plants a tree whose shade they will never sit beneath. You can either continue to sit back and hope that we don't destroy ourselves, or you can finally do your jobs and begin building a future that is peaceful and secure for all.

So, what will it be? Thank you.

Statement by the Egyptian Council for Foreign Affairs
Speaker: Ambassador Dr. Mohamed Mounir Zahran

Madam Chair,

The Egyptian Council for Foreign Affairs (ECFA) was established in Cairo, Egypt, with the objective of attaining a deep understanding of all foreign affairs issues at both regional and international levels. ECFA is a co-author of and fully endorses the NGO New Agenda Coalition Statement delivered before this session of the NPT Review Conference and the Joint Statement delivered on 28 April 2015 by Austria on the Humanitarian Consequences of Nuclear Weapons. However, I am delivering the following statement on behalf of the civil society and NGOs in Egypt with a focus on some important issues regarding the present NPT Review Conference, particularly issues related to the Middle East.

Unfortunately, the NPT did not yield the expected results since its entry into force in 1970 and since its indefinite extension. It also failed to establish a Zone Free of Nuclear Weapons and other Weapons of Mass Destruction [in the Middle East], without which the 1995 decision of the NPT Indefinite Extension would not have been adopted. We are also alarmed by the failure to implement the outcomes of the 2000 and 2010 NPT Review Conferences, as it is stated in the full statement which is available in ECFA's website www.ecfa-egypt.org.

Due to the shortcomings of the treaty implementation, we call for the following:

1. The 2015 Review Conference is being convened in the shadow of several failures. The first is the non-implementation of the 1995 Resolution on the Middle East, which was a pre-condition for the indefinite Treaty extension and part of a package of the 1995 Review Conference's decision to implement the outcome of the 2000

and 2010 Review Conferences and in particular convening the 2012 Helsinki Conference on the Middle East.

2. At the 9th Review Conference in New York, the Arab Countries submitted a paper which echoed support from the Non-Aligned Movement (NAM) and requested the UN Secretary General to convene a Conference on the Middle East Zone within 180 days after the end of the Review Conference.

3. In the aftermath of the failure of the last NPT Review Conference, we are keen to save the future of the NPT and the non-proliferation regime. Hence we propose that the UN Secretary General invite all Middle East countries that have not yet done so, including Israel, to accede to Weapons of Mass Destruction (WMD) Treaties, namely the NPT, BWC and/or CWC and deposit such instruments with the Security Council through the UN Secretary General.

4. In order to ensure the credibility of the NPT, including the implementation of Article VI and comply with the 1996 ICJ Advisory Opinion, a legally binding multilateral nuclear disarmament treaty should be negotiated in the framework of the Conference on Disarmament (CD). Such a treaty shall ensure a universal, non-discriminatory regime of a nuclear-weapon-free world as required by the UN General Assembly in its relevant resolutions, the latest being Resolution 69/29.

5. It is worth noting that achieving nuclear disarmament by a legally binding international instrument will make the ME zone redundant. Thus, an immediate launch of negotiations should take place, without any further delay, to conclude an international convention that totally eliminates nuclear weapons in the world by prohibiting their production, acquisition, development, stockpiling, testing, transfer, use or threat of use, and stipulates their total destruction and elimination from the planet within a time-bound frame.

6. Nuclear Weapons States (NWS) must stop pressuring the Non-Nuclear Weapons States (NNWS) that opt to exercise their inalienable right to enrich uranium for the peaceful uses of nuclear energy, in conformity with Article IV of the NPT treaty, in order to regain confidence in the non-proliferation regime.

7.   Nuclear Weapons States (NWS) must fully abide by their obligations derived from Article I and VI of the NPT. Thus, NWS should desist from their policy of nuclear sharing with NNWS or States that did not accede to the NPT, namely, DPRK, India, Israel and Pakistan.

8.   The considerable financial spending currently dedicated to nuclear weapons and their maintenance should be mobilized and devoted to support peace, security and sustainable development, together with the realization of dignified life for all human beings and the welfare of humanity.

9.   Bearing in mind the shortcomings in the implementation of the Treaty, particularly nuclear disarmament and the non-implementation of the establishment of a nuclear-weapon-free zone in the Middle East, we are convinced that the 1995 decision on the indefinite extension of the Treaty should be revisited in the 2015 NPT Review Conference and be replaced by another decision which extends the Treaty for five years subject to periodical reviews.

10.   Against this background including the failure of the last NPT Review Conference, we are convinced that the 1995 decision on the Indefinite Extension of the Treaty should be reviewed through a common position to be taken in all fora, regional, as well as international including in the UN General Assembly. In order to avert an institutional vacuum, that decision should be replaced by another decision to be adopted by a majority vote to extend the treaty every five years subject to its regular review.

Statement by the International Association of Lawyers Against Nuclear Arms
Speaker: Peter Weiss, Co-President

Nuclear Disarmament: The Fierce Urgency of Now

Madam President, Your Excellencies, Ladies and Gentlemen, my name is Peter Weiss and I am Co-President of IALANA, the International Association of Lawyers Against Nuclear Arms. I call your attention to our paper, "Nuclear Disarmament: The Road Ahead", which is available outside this room. It contains our legal analysis of the nuclear weapons issue and our recommendations for going forward.

But I want to speak to you today more as a citizen of this endangered world than as a lawyer. I had the privilege of addressing an NPT Review Conference once before, in 2000. Not a great deal has changed since then, except that I am 15 years older and approaching my 90th birthday. I therefore have an urgent request to put before you, dear distinguished delegates: Make the nuclear weapons free world happen, which, to listen to their speeches, all world leaders desire, but make it happen in my lifetime.

It should not be difficult. You, more than any other body, have the power to do it. Every long march requires a first step. This conference should end with a decision to launch a process to start drafting a convention or treaty that will define the path leading to the total elimination of the thousands of nuclear weapons that now threaten a catastrophe of unimaginable proportions. That path should be subject to effective verification and be completed within a reasonable, fixed time line.

Oslo, Nayarit and Vienna have demonstrated that continuing the nuclear arms race is the devil's work, while a child could understand that a world without nuclear weapons is infinitely preferable to one in which such weapons exist; The failure to take a first step toward total nuclear disarmament can only be understood as unwillingness to embark on the road to zero.

The nuclear weapons story has had its heroes. The Hibakusha who keep the memory of Hiroshima and Nagasaki alive so that no one else will ever have to suffer as they did; Lt. Col. Petrov, who paid with the loss of his career for refusing to carry out a procedure that could have plunged the world into nuclear holocaust; the tiny Republic of the Marshall Islands which has taken all nine nuclear armed states to the International Court of Justice for their failure to carry out their disarmament obligation; Sister Megan Rice, the 85 year old nun who is spending three years in prison for pouring some of her own blood on the wall of a building housing enough weapons grade uranium to manufacture thousands of nuclear weapons.

What we need now is a heroic state, or coalition of states, who will risk the displeasure of the powerful nuclear weapon states by leading the way to a world not just free of, but liberated from, the curse of nuclear weapons. I have faith that such states are represented in this chamber today. But please remember: in my lifetime.

Statement by the International Campaign to Abolish Nuclear Weapons

Speaker: Daniela Verano

The humanitarian initiative began here five years ago, when the NPT Review Conference expressed its deep concern at the catastrophic humanitarian consequences of nuclear weapons.

Since then, a fundamental shift has been under way.

Concerns about the impact of nuclear weapons on people and the environment have become central to disarmament discussions.

There is a new sense of empowerment among the peoples and the governments of countries that reject nuclear weapons.

There is a new sense of discomfort among the governments of nuclear-armed states and their allies.

There is a new and growing expectation that negotiations are going to begin in the near term on a legally binding instrument to ban nuclear weapons.

So, in one way, we are greatly encouraged by the progress since governments last gathered in this format in 2010.

Unfortunately, the states that wield nuclear weapons have not kept pace with this progress.

On the contrary, they have protested every step of the way that the humanitarian initiative is a distraction from what they see as the real work of nuclear disarmament.

They have protested that such discussions should not take place without them, while initially choosing to stay away from the meetings themselves.

This opposition has been revealing.

It reveals a concern that discussions about the unacceptable consequences of nuclear weapons will inevitably lead to their international prohibition.

It reveals a concern that the relentless multi-billion dollar modernisation of nuclear arsenals is being exposed through international discussions.

It reveals a concern that an initiative is emerging and can move forward even without the nuclear-armed states.

This is our main message today—that we can and we must move forward with a ban, with or without the nuclear-armed states.

There is an opportunity before us—as an international community—to prohibit nuclear weapons.

We should not let it slip through our hands.

We should not accept a framing that such a prohibition is impossible. It is not. It is already clearly under discussion, it is consistent with the disarmament goals and principles of the NPT and with the broader development of international law, and it is coming.

We should not accept a framing that such a prohibition would make no difference. The fact that the nuclear-armed states oppose it should tell us that it's a meaningful pursuit that will challenge their possession of nuclear weapons.

We should not accept a framing that such a prohibition is polarising or divisive. Adopting a new international legal standard to prohibit nuclear weapons is a responsibility.

Not all states will join at the same time. That is not divisive, that is the nature of international agreements.

Those who oppose negotiations towards a ban on nuclear weapons are in danger of giving support to the nuclear-armed states in their efforts to control the discourse on nuclear weapons.

The world is now well set to begin these negotiations.

The focus on the humanitarian impact of nuclear weapons is the right starting point. It leads directly to a conclusion that prohibiting nuclear weapons is the right next step.

The pledge that so many governments have made to fill the legal gap on the prohibition and elimination of nuclear weapons has demonstrated clearly the willingness of states to start work on a new legally binding instrument.

The focus on effective measures here at the NPT, is an expression of that work towards a legally binding instrument.

Negotiations should commence this year—the year which marks the 70th anniversary of the atomic bombing of Hiroshima and Nagasaki.

The ban treaty and the process of work to put it in place will not immediately solve all the problems with nuclear weapons.

Nor are these efforts meant to replace the work to reduce nuclear arsenals and maintain dialogue among nuclear-armed states on disarmament.

All of these efforts must intensify. They are not mutually exclusive, but mutually reinforcing.

The ban treaty has an irresistible logic.

We can see already from the statements here this week that many states are embracing that logic and signalling a clear determination to act upon it.

Through our campaign partners in 95 countries, the International Campaign to Abolish Nuclear Weapons will be there to support states through these negotiations every step of the way.

So let's start.

Statement by the Mayor of Hiroshima

Speaker: Kazumi Matsui

It is an honor for me to address delegates and non-governmental groups attending this 2015 NPT Review Conference.

On this year, which marks the 70th anniversary of the first atomic bombing in the history of humanity, many citizens including the atomic bomb survivors (*hibakusha*) from Hiroshima and Nagasaki have gathered here in New York City with a strong wish for the presentation of a concrete roadmap for nuclear weapons abolition at this conference. Today, representing the atomic bombed cities of Hiroshima and Nagasaki, and as the president of Mayors for Peace, an organization consisting of over 6,600 like-minded member cities from 160 countries and regions around the world, I would like to say a few words.

At 8:15 a.m. on August 6, 1945, the single atomic bomb dropped on Hiroshima reduced the city to ruin through the massive radiation and fierce heat rays and blast that it released, killing indiscriminately non-combatants like women, children, and the elderly, who accounted for the vast majority of the 350,000 people who were in Hiroshima at the time. The number of those who perished as a result of the atomic bombing reached approximately 140,000 by the end of 1945.

Furthermore, those who just barely managed to survive have been tormented by lifelong suffering, such as the sorrow of losing their families and friends, the long-term effects of the radiation, and concerns about their health. Even now, 70 years after the atomic bombing, the survivors continue to suffer from deep wounds on their bodies and souls.

Seeing the reality of the atomic bombing, it is clear that nuclear weapons are ultimate inhumane weapons, and are an absolute evil.

For some seven decades now, the *hibakusha* have been recounting their experiences. Having experienced indescribable suffering, they have arrived at their unshakable conviction that "no one shall ever again suffer as we have", and continue to spread the inhumane impacts of the atomic bombing to the world, ringing the alarm bell. Appealing that the only way to guarantee that nuclear weapons are never used again is the total elimination of nuclear weapons, they have been putting in their best efforts towards the realization of a world without nuclear weapons. Mayors for Peace gives full support to this earnest appeal of the *hibakusha*.

In this context, I note with acclaim that both the 2000 and 2010 NPT Review Conferences adopted consensus language referring to nuclear disarmament as offering the only "absolute guarantee" against any future use—or threat of use—of such weapons. I also welcome the fact that the 2010 Review Conference voiced its deep concern at the continued risks posed for humanity by the possible use of these weapons and the catastrophic humanitarian consequences that would result, and referred to a nuclear weapons convention.

I am similarly encouraged by the impressive attendance at the three major international conferences that have been held in recent years in Norway, Mexico, and Austria on the humanitarian consequences of nuclear weapons. These conferences included opportunities to hear testimonies from the *hibakusha*, which encouraged the resolution for nuclear weapons abolition among the participants even further. Through these conferences, the participants deepened their awareness about the inhumanity of nuclear weapons, as well as on the risks that nuclear weapons may actually be used as a result of misunderstanding or accident. Additionally, the recognition that nuclear weapons have absolutely no role to play in maintaining international peace, is widely being shared. Currently, many of the governments attending these conferences are working closely with civil society to advance this humanitarian approach.

Some people, however, insist that nuclear weapons abolition requires a security environment that will make this possible. Mayors for Peace, an organization of which I serve as president, not only appeals for nuclear weapons abolition, but is urging the governments of various nations to shift from the security system relying on "nuclear deterrence" based on mutual distrust and threat, to a more humane and sustainable security system. And, in support of such a shift, we work hard with wide-ranging civil society partners to cultivate a shared sense of world community rooted in an awareness that we all belong to the same human family. This way of thinking is in line with the principles of the Charter of the United Nations, such as the elimination of all sorts of weapons of mass destruction, a reduction in military expenditures, the prohibition of threat or use of force. The member cities of Mayors for Peace, supporting this cause, have increased by approximately 2,000 cities in even just the past four years of my term as mayor, and this number continues to increase at an accelerating rate. Currently, the population of all these cities makes up one-seventh of the total population of the world, and like-minded citizens around the world are increasing even further.

Others claim that mutual distrust among nations and the existence of terrorists are impeding nuclear disarmament. However, we of Mayors for Peace cannot agree with this assertion. When so many sensible people from all across the civil society are struggling hard to promote mutual understanding among international society, in the aim for a peaceful world without nuclear weapons, what is the significance of political leadership? It is now the time for the policymakers of the world, especially those of nuclear weapon states, to demonstrate decisive leadership and work together towards nuclear weapons abolition and the creation of an international environment that will make it possible. The *hibakusha*, Mayors for Peace, and various like-minded groups in the civil society around the world will give full support to such political leadership, and are willing to work together to achieve it.

Consolidated efforts by state and city governments, parliamentarians, women, youth, scholars, lawyers, doctors, artists, environmentalists, human rights activists, and countless other constituencies can change the world.

I would therefore like to appeal to everyone participating in the current NPT Review Conference to work together to achieve a successful outcome. In this regard, I am convinced that the realization of a nuclear-weapon-free world will require a nuclear weapons convention or some other legal framework with the same goal.

Article VI of the NPT requires not only nuclear weapons states but also all its parties to pursue negotiations in good faith on nuclear disarmament. However, wide legal gap still remains towards the total prohibition of nuclear weapons even after the 45-year history of the NPT. Now is the time at this conference that the NPT Parties agree to begin negotiations to close this legal gap and, in particular, to start negotiation on a nuclear weapons convention at the earliest possible time.

In conclusion, I strongly urge the representatives of all the states parties to the NPT to unite and make significant steps forward toward nuclear weapons abolition at this 2015 Review Conference, and let us never give up in the pursuit of this great cause until it is finally achieved. On our part, we, Mayors for Peace, together with wide-ranging civil society partners will do everything that we can.

Statement by the Mayor of Nagasaki
Speaker: Tomihisa Taue

Chairman Ambassador Taous Feroukhi, distinguished delegates and leaders of civil groups,

My name is Tomihisa Taue, the Mayor of Nagasaki. It is an honor to address you today as the representative of Nagasaki, a city which was devastated by an atomic bomb, and as the Vice-President of Mayors for Peace.

Seventy years ago, on the 9th of August 1945, Nagasaki became the world's second city to be attacked by an atomic bomb. The terrible heat rays, blast, and radiation released by the atomic bomb instantly destroyed the city, and caused 150,000 civilian casualties. These included children and the elderly. Even today, those who narrowly survived are still suffering from the aftereffects of radiation exposure.

Today, many *hibakusha*, atomic bomb survivors, are using the last of their strength to be here in New York to appeal for the abolition of nuclear weapons. This year, the average age of the *hibakusha* will be 80. There is not much time left to them. We have a responsibility to show these survivors the path to the abolition of nuclear weapons while they are alive to witness it.

The "Conference on the Humanitarian Impact of Nuclear Weapons" has been held three times since the 2010 NPT Review Conference. We have arrived at this NPT Review Conference amid rising debate surrounding nuclear disarmament, thanks to the focus being placed on their inhumanity. However, far from the articles of the previous Review Conference's Final Document being honored, we see a return to the Cold War era. Nuclear war is ever more likely as tensions rise between Russia and the U.S.A. over the political turmoil in Ukraine. At this rate, the NPT regime is in danger of becoming a mere façade.

I ask the following of the nuclear weapon states:

Firstly, I urge the U.S.A and Russia to speed up their nuclear arms reduction. We would see progress in nuclear disarmament negotiations between all five nuclear weapon states if both the U.S.A and Russia were to reduce their nuclear arsenal to 500 warheads.

Last month, Ambassador Feroukhi visited Hiroshima and Nagasaki. I would like to ask not only heads of state and heads of government, but all those involved in the nuclear problem, to come to Hiroshima and Nagasaki. There, you will see the truth of exposure to nuclear weapons with your own eyes. If you do, you will understand just how inhumane these weapons are, and also understand that we must be rid of them as soon as possible.

I appeal to the non-nuclear states that are under nuclear umbrellas:

Please recall Action 1 of the 2010 NPT Review Conference Final Document which states that:

"All States parties commit to pursue policies that are fully compatible with the Treaty and the objective of achieving a world without nuclear weapons."

I ask that you obey these terms which you have each sworn to, and be aware that this is a problem faced by each and every one of us.

One of these policies we must pursue is the creation of "Nuclear Weapon Free Zones". Instead of nuclear umbrellas, we must expand the range of "non-nuclear umbrellas". For those of us living in northeast Asia, there is tension concerning North Korea's nuclear capabilities. I ask that Japan, for the sake of a stable northeast Asia, approach South Korea and North Korea and make efforts to establish a "Northeast Asia Nuclear Weapon Free Zone".

I address the non-nuclear states that are not relying on nuclear deterrence:

I thank the many of you who are forming nuclear weapon free zones. I hope that your strong cooperation will finally set in motion the creation of a "Middle East Weapons of Mass Destruction Free Zone". Furthermore, I ask for your continued activity so that we can make all 7.2 billion global citizens participate in the international discourse concerning the inhumanity of nuclear weapons.

Many countries have submitted working documents to today's Review Conference to promote nuclear disarmament. Our goal is the same, even if our approaches towards the abolition of nuclear weapons differ. We should use this Conference to create a new and continuing conference which is open to all countries, where we can create a road map towards our goal.

I ask each of you to acknowledge that while we have been unable to rid ourselves of our old-fashioned reliance on nuclear deterrence, the danger has once again grown. 70 years after the atomic bombings, let us make this Review Conference a turning point in the creation of a new world which denies the value of nuclear weapons.

I look forward to a lively discussion at the NPT Review Conference, and hope that you will achieve the progress desired by the *hibakusha*.

Thank you very much.

Statement by the Group of Non-Governmental Experts from Countries Belonging to the New Agenda Coalition[1]
Speaker: Alyn Ware

Introduction

The Group of non-governmental experts from the New Agenda Coalition (NAC) countries was established in 2007 in order to support the efforts of the NAC and to offer input for the promotion of nuclear disarmament and non-proliferation with a particular focus on the Treaty on the Non-Proliferation of Nuclear Weapons' (NPT) Review cycles. The NAC-NGO group collaborates inter-sessionally and has on a number of occasions—particularly during the period leading up to the 2010 Review Conference and this current Review Process—outlined its common views and has made recommendations for enhancing and strengthening the global disarmament and non-proliferation regime.

The NAC-NGO Group continues to strongly believe in the importance of the NPT and its three pillars. We recognise that at present the NPT represents the only binding commitment in a multilateral treaty to the goal of disarmament. We also, unfortunately, recognise that Nuclear Weapon States Parties have failed to make significant progress towards achieving this particular objective. The obligation to pursue in "good faith and bring to a conclusion

---

[1] Drafted and submitted by Ambassador Mohamed I Shaker, Ambassador Abdel Raouf El Reedy, Dr M. Mounir Zahran and Ambassador Mahmoud Karem representing the Egyptian Council for Foreign Affairs (Egypt); Mr Tony D'Costa, Pax Christi and International Catholic Peace Movement (Ireland); Mr Fernando Solana, Mexican Council on Foreign Relations (Mexico); Mr Alyn Ware, The Peace Foundation Disarmament and Security Centre (New Zealand); Mr Noel Stott, Institute for Security Studies (South Africa).

negotiations leading to nuclear disarmament in all its aspects under strict and effective international control" has not yet been achieved.

As citizens of countries that are committed to not develop nuclear weapons in exchange for existing nuclear weapons states agreeing to eliminate their own stocks of nuclear weapons—the bargain we struck 45 years ago—we call on these latter States to honour their unequivocal undertaking to disarm under article VI of the NPT. At the same time, we would be remiss not to remind all States Parties present here that Article VI of the NPT stipulates that "each of the Parties to the Treaty undertakes to pursue negotiations in good faith on effective measures relating to cessation of the nuclear arms race at an early date and to nuclear disarmament, and on a treaty on general and complete disarmament under strict and effective international control". It is thus the responsibility of all NPT States Parties and not just those that continue to maintain their stockpiles and who continue to improve their explosive power.

The current discourse on the catastrophic humanitarian impact of nuclear detonations, whether by design, intent or accident as reflected in the outcomes of the Oslo, Nayarit and Vienna conferences, has once again highlighted the vital importance to prohibit nuclear weapons, achieve complete nuclear disarmament, prevent proliferation, and ensure that nuclear technology is only used for peaceful purposes. This reinforces the International Court of Justice Advisory Opinion of July 1996 which concluded that the threat or use of nuclear weapons would generally violate international humanitarian law and that there is an unconditional obligation to achieve complete nuclear disarmament.

If the NPT is unable to deliver *all* of its objectives, and not just two of its pillars however important they are, then the sad truth is that another forum or regime needs to be established—a forum and regime that will place the humanitarian impact of nuclear weapons detonations and the security imperative for nuclear abolition, at the core of all its deliberations.

This NPT Review Conference occurs on the 70th anniversary of the war-time use of nuclear weapons against Hiroshima and Nagasaki, and 20 years since the NPT was indefinitely extended to allow more time for states to implement their commitment to the "cessation of the nuclear arms race at an early date" and "to nuclear disarmament."

However, indefinite extension of the NPT is not a licence for the nuclear weapon States to continue their nuclear doctrines indefinitely. Indeed, the case lodged by the Marshall Islands in the International Court of Justice against the nuclear weapon States calls correctly for time-bound implementation of the disarmament obligation.

Proposals in a variety of multilateral fora, along with statements/resolutions by inter-parliamentary organisations, religious leaders & interfaith organisations, humanitarian organisations including the International Committee of the Red Cross (ICRC), city mayors and many civil society organisations, elevate the political imperative for countries with nuclear weapons to read the signs of the times and respond to them by agreeing to a process for the complete prohibition and elimination of nuclear weapons.

Such multilateral fora include the UN open-ended working group to "develop proposals to take forward multilateral nuclear disarmament negotiations for the achievement and maintenance of a world without nuclear weapons"; the High-Level Meeting of the UN General Assembly on Nuclear Disarmament on 26 September 2013, which concluded with an overwhelming majority of countries condemning the continued existence of nuclear weapons and expressing support for a comprehensive convention on nuclear weapons that would "remove the scourge of these weapons of terror once and for all"; the joint statements on the humanitarian impact of nuclear weapons delivered by more than 150 governments to the United Nations General Assembly's First Committee on Peace and International Security; as well as the 2014 General Assembly which adopted resolution 69/37 urging this forum to explore options for the elaboration of effective measures as envisaged and required by Article VI of the NPT.

As stated by Pope Francis, in his message to the December Vienna Conference on the Humanitarian Impact of Nuclear Weapons, "If it is unthinkable to imagine a world where nuclear weapons are available to all, it is reasonable to imagine a world where nobody has them", or as the UK's Church of England Bishops have stated, "shifts in the global strategic realities mean that the traditional arguments for nuclear deterrence need re-examining [and that] the presence of such destructive capacity pulls against any international sense of shared community".

NPT States Parties need to be open and transparent about what steps they will take to achieve and maintain a nuclear-weapon-free world. States Parties therefore need to urgently give concrete effect to their unequivocal commitment to eliminate nuclear weapons in light of their unacceptable humanitarian consequences and associated risks and "follow the imperative of human security for all and to promote the protection of civilians against risks stemming from nuclear weapons". Concrete measures with clearly defined benchmarks and timelines are required so as to illustrate that the achievement and maintenance of a world without nuclear weapons is not just an illusion created by the nuclear-weapon States to contain any possible breakouts out of the NPT. Such steps would restore confidence in the NPT and reinforce the global norms towards a more peaceful and secure future for all without the perpetual threat of annihilation.

The Resolution on the Middle East

The fact that the Helsinki process has not yielded any significant results is not only sad but in many senses unacceptable. Unacceptable because despite arduous negotiations during the 2010 Review Cycle between concerned delegations particularly the Egyptian and US delegations and the appointment of a facilitator from Finland by the UN Secretary General, the holding of a Conference did not happen in 2012, as was agreed, and has still not been held.

The withdrawal from the Second Preparatory Committee for the 2015 Review Conference in April 2013 of the delegation from Egypt is therefore understandable. However, this not only leaves the future of this Review Conference at risk, it also once again calls into question the integrity and future of the NPT as a whole. It should be recalled by all that the Middle East Resolution was a primary basis without which the decision on the 1995 indefinite extension of the NPT would not have been adopted—in fact the adoption of a resolution on the establishment of a Middle East WMD free zone was a necessary condition for the decision to indefinitely extend the Treaty. It is understandable, therefore, and of concern that the non-implementation of this resolution and the package of decisions taken in 1995 could lead to some State Parties questioning the validity of the indefinite extension and the credibility of NPT commitments themselves.

We highlight the recent call by the League of Arab States to the UN Secretary General to pursue the efforts to convene this conference with renewed vigour with a view to ensuring its success.

Conclusion

- We share the conviction that the total elimination of nuclear weapons is the only guarantee against the use, or threat of use, of such weapons either by States or non-State actors;

- We support, in particular, the proposals for achieving and implementing a global agreement or package of agreements to prohibit and eliminate nuclear weapons;

- We appreciate and fully support the New Agenda Coalition (NAC) as a champion of nuclear disarmament and therefore commend to all NPT States Parties, nuclear armed states outside of the NPT as well as global civil society, NAC's working papers to the 2014 NPT Preparatory Committee meeting on nuclear disarmament, humanitarian consequences and the fulfilment of Article VI of the NPT as well as the more recent March 2015 (NPT/CONF.2015/WP.9) working paper on Article VI of the Treaty on the Non-Proliferation of Nuclear Weapons;

- We call on NPT States parties to agree to commence a diplomatic process, open to all UN member states, to commence deliberations and negotiations on nuclear disarmament, drawing upon the options proposed in the OEWG and to the NPT including those contained in the NAC working papers (NPT/CONF.2015/PC.III/WP.18 and NPT/CONF.2015/WP.9).

- We encourage the New Agenda Coalition and other countries engaged in the humanitarian consequences dimension to continue the series of international conferences which have elevated the humanitarian imperative for nuclear abolition, and to focus the next conference on the challenge of Austria to fill the legal gap for nuclear abolition by exploring and developing the legal options to achieve this.

Statement by Parliamentarians for Nuclear Non-Proliferation and Disarmament
Speaker: Phil Goff, Member of Parliament and Chair, New Zealand PNND

United Nations Secretary-General Ban Ki-moon said, "There are no right hands for wrong weapons." The overwhelming majority of countries agree. Yet the nuclear weapons States tells us that they have the rights, the hands and the need to possess these weapons of mass destruction. We all know that human hands are fallible. Indeed, the risks and consequences of a nuclear weapon detonation are too serious for this meeting to result in failure. These risks are heightened through the new risk of cyber warfare and the growth of terrorist groups.

We all know that if some States insist on a so-called right to nuclear weapons, it is illogical to expect that others won't also expect similar "rights". It's a recipe for proliferation.

As for the need for nuclear weapons, we in New Zealand can understand how such a belief can arise in a dangerous world. We too used to be under the nuclear umbrella but we cast away its myth that threatening to annihilate civilians provides security—and since abolishing nuclear weapons our security has arguably improved, and our international status and influence have been enhanced.

It is more than half a century since US President John F. Kennedy evocatively declared that a country using nuclear weapons would fail to protect its own people—"Even the fruits of victory would be ashes in our mouths!"

This is no less true today. At least 159 countries have signed up to an initiative on the humanitarian consequences of the use of nuclear weapons. These are so grave—the destruction of civilisation and humanity—that their use, possession and development should be prohibited. The only way to protect ourselves against that risk is for all nuclear weapons to be eliminated.

To protect people against a nuclear holocaust all Parties to the NPT must meet their obligations under the Treaty. Most of us have done so—we have not proliferated nuclear weapons. We have met our side of the bargain. Those who possess nuclear weapons promised as the quid pro quo 45 years ago that they too would disarm.

The P5 have not met their side of the bargain under Article VI, despite solemnly agreeing to do so. Unequivocal undertakings have been made and repeated but not implemented and honoured.

The US and Russia maintain over 1,000 weapons on Cold War high alert status and under launch-on-warning policies. Rescinding this would be a straightforward and effective step towards making the world safer. Some have still not ratified the CTBT. The nuclear weapon states are spending US$100 billion a year on their nuclear weapons, much of that to modernise them.

Their continued development of strategies based on the possession and potential use of nuclear weapons cannot be reconciled with Article VI obligations to disarm.

If they do not agree at this NPT to concrete, detailed measures to phase out nuclear deterrence and eliminate their stockpiles, then non-nuclear States will most likely look for other mechanisms outside the NPT to address this.

Parliamentarians for Non-Proliferation and Disarmament urge governments in the coming 3 weeks to make the historic breakthrough that the world has been awaiting for nearly half a century.

The Inter Parliamentary Union, which comprises the parliaments of over 160 countries including the parliaments of most of the nuclear-armed States, last year adopted a resolution by consensus calling on their governments to eliminate the role of nuclear weapons in security doctrines, and to negotiate a nuclear weapons convention or package of agreements.

What this Conference must deliver is progress on the implementation of Article VI of the Non-Proliferation Treaty—on the development of a comprehensive legally-binding mechanism for the achievement and maintenance of a world without nuclear weapons. The disarmament pillar of the Treaty must be given the same focus as the nonproliferation pillar.

Let the legacy of this Conference not be continued apathy and complacency about this threat but a determined commitment that nations act upon to ensure the survival of humanity.

Statement by the Peace and Planet Mobilization for a Nuclear-Free, Peaceful, Just and Sustainable World
Speaker: Jackie Cabasso, United for Peace and Justice

The Peace and Planet Mobilization for a Nuclear-Free, Peaceful, Just and Sustainable World emerged out of last year's Annual General Meeting of the Abolition 2000 Global Network to Eliminate Nuclear Weapons. Looking ahead at that time to the Vienna Conference on the Humanitarian Impact of Nuclear Weapons, we discussed and debated "what comes next." We recognized the deep flaws in the NPT and the failure of the NPT Review process to move us closer to a world without nuclear weapons. But we nonetheless saw the importance of a strong, visible civil society presence at the 2015 Review Conference that would bring a clarion call for negotiations to begin immediately on the elimination of nuclear weapons.

Peace and Planet was organized by an International Planning Group made up of representatives from 11 international organizations and 43 organizations based in 12 countries.

We issued our Call to Action on September 26, 2014, the first International Day for the Total Elimination of Nuclear Weapons, urging "all people who hope to build a fair, democratic, ecologically sustainable and peaceful future to join us in New York City and around the world for international days of action" on the eve of the NPT Review Conference. It reads, in part:

> We issue this call at a crucial juncture in history, a moment when the unresolved tensions of a deeply inequitable society, great power ambitions and the destructive effects of an unsustainable economic system are exploding into overlapping crises. Tensions among nuclear-armed countries are rising amidst circumstances that bear worrisome resemblances to those that brought the world wars of the last century. For the first time in the nuclear age we are in a sustained global economic crisis

that is deepening the gulf between rich and poor in a starkly two-tier world. Both climate change and fossil fuel-based economies generate conflicts within and among states. Extreme economic inequality and the economic policies that create it, NATO's aggressive expansion, struggles over diminishing fossil fuels, food price spikes and crop failures drive wars and revive arms races from Iraq to Syria to Ukraine to South Asia and the Western Pacific. We face a moment in which policies that benefit a fraction of the world's population feed conflicts that could precipitate catastrophic wars, even nuclear wars, and in which the power to make war is wielded by largely unaccountable elites.

The Call to Action also highlighted the challenge in the International Court of Justice initiated a year ago by the Republic of the Marshall Islands, urging the ICJ to find the nine nuclear-armed states in noncompliance with their obligations to disarm under international law:

This courageous action by direct victims of nuclear colonialism reminds us that disarmament depends on collective action by the people of the world, using all available peaceful means. We urge governments of non-nuclear weapons States to participate by intervening in the Marshall Islands cases or by filing their own parallel applications.

The Peace and Planet Mobilization was endorsed by a diverse array of 353 organizations in 20 countries, including faith-based groups, organizations dedicated to peace and disarmament, development, social justice, climate change and environmental issues and organizations of social workers, educators and academics, scientists and engineers, women, labor, youth, veterans and lawyers—a testament to our common vision.

Peace and Planet weekend opened Friday evening, April 24, with an international conference in the historic Cooper Union Hall. On Friday and Saturday, 600 participants heard from hibakusha, scholars, parliamentarians, mayors and leading activists, meeting in plenaries and workshops to explore ways to weave our issues together and strengthen our movement.

Sunday, April 26, began with an interfaith convocation followed by a rally in Union Square. Seated in front were 80 hibakusha. The high point was the launch of the "Global Peace Wave." At the appointed time, giant cardboard cut-out hands were raised and people as far as the eye could see "waved goodbye to nuclear weapons." The Global Wave went westward, by time zone, with more than 100 actions around the world, arriving back at the UN 24 hours later for the opening of the Review Conference.

From the rally, 7,500 people marched to Dag Hammarskjöld Plaza carrying colorful signs and banners, singing and chanting. Over 1,000 people had come from Japan, and 90 from France. Others came from Germany, the Marshall Islands, Korea, Norway, Sweden, the UK, Scotland, Cameroon, Brazil, Nepal, the Netherlands, Canada, Kazakhstan, Belgium, Lithuania, the Philippines, the Czech Republic and Greece, and from across the United States.

At Dag Hammarskjöld Plaza, the crowd was greeted by UN High Representative for Disarmament Affairs, Angela Kane, and Ambassador Taous Feroukhi, President of the 2015 Review Conference, who graciously accepted over 7 million signatures on petitions collected by Gensuikyo (the Japan Council Against A and H Bombs), Mayors for Peace, and Peace and Planet. Our message is clear:

- We call upon the parties to the NPT to use the 2015 Review Conference to immediately, without delay, develop a timetable to ban and eliminate all nuclear weapons.

- We call upon the four states outside the Treaty that have nuclear arms, India, Israel, North Korea, and Pakistan, to join this process, immediately and without delay.

We say: Yes to a Nuclear-Free World! Yes to Nonviolence! Yes to Economic Justice and Environmental Sustainability! Yes to Peace!!

Statement by People for Nuclear Disarmament/Human Survival Project
Speaker: John Hallam

I have six minutes.

Six minutes is around the same time that a commander of missile forces, a defense minister, or a President, has to decide, after a 30 second briefing (for the US President) whether or not to launch about 2,000 nuclear warheads (around 900 on alert in silos in the US and Russia, plus submarine-based warheads) as early warning systems indicate—likely incorrectly—that the other "side" has launched.

If it is indeed true that the other "side" has launched, then it is indeed the end of what we know as "the world". If (as is quite probable) the incoming missiles are merely a computer glitch, and "our" side launches anyway, it will just as surely be the "end of the world" as the "other side"—if acting in accordance with "deterrence" theory—will certainly launch in response, making our belief that the end of the world has arrived self-fulfilling.

Even if the other side does NOT launch in response, the smoke from "their" burning cities will still make "OUR" country (and the rest of the world) uninhabitable, inducing global famine lasting for decades. (Self-Assured destruction by Alan Robock, BAS) A conflagration involving US/NATO forces and those of Russia would most likely cause the deaths of most humans (and severely impact/ extinguish other species) as well as destroying the delicate interwoven techno-structure on which latter-day "civilization" has come to depend. Human survival itself could be arguably problematic under a 2,000+ warhead US/Russia scenario, though human ingenuity and resilience shouldn't be underestimated.

The destruction of the information-based techno-structure and the complete disappearance of the global financial system could be accomplished with a very few large warheads (such as the Chinese

DF5, of 5Mt) exploded in space, with the effects of Electromagnetic Pulse (in fact results of EMP can also be duplicated by a very large coronal mass ejection such as took place in 1859. A study by the US Congress indicates that in either event, up to 90% of US citizens might starve to death. This, without the destruction of a single city. Most studies say that electronic systems in the entire continental US could be crippled by just one large warhead exploded about 400 Km out in space.)

Even a "boutique" India/Pakistan nuclear exchange, involving 100-200 Hiroshima-sized warheads, could put of up to 2 billion people worldwide at risk of death from famine.

But just how likely really is such a scenario? Surely it's just science-fiction with which NGOs frighten roomfuls of diplomats? How likely really is a completely catastrophic event-sequence?

Firstly, as I'm relatively innumerate and am not Seth Baum (who will be presenting with me at a panel on 6 May at 1 pm), or Prof. Martin Hellman, on both of whose highly numerate analyses I have largely depended, I am not going to try to give you a number which anyway may not be that meaningful. But some common-sense things can be said nonetheless about catastrophic nuclear risk.

- Risk is not simply a function of the probability of a given event, but is a function of probability times consequences, or "$r = p \times c$".

  This means that even if the probability of a global nuclear exchange is relatively low, the consequences are so grave that only a probability of zero or very close thereto can be acceptable.

- Even if the probability of an accidental apocalypse seems reasonably low (say, 0.1%-1%) in any given year, if this is taken over an indefinitely large number of years, the risk approaches asymptotically to 100%.

- Nuclear risk has PALPABLY increased in the last 2-3 years, with the most obvious indicators being the movement of the hands of the *Bulletin of Atomic Scientists* "Doomsday Clock" from five minutes to three minutes to midnight. In addition there have been a series of articles on nuclear war risks and nuclear deterrence in *Der Spiegel* (arguing that nuclear war risks now are HIGHER than during the cold war), *The Guardian*, *Foreign Affairs*, *The Economist*, and others. The clearest driver of increased risk is of course, the current crisis in Ukraine, with the associated nuclear threats. Even to make such threats in and of itself arguably considerably increases risk.

– Minuteman missile forces and Russian strategic rocket forces (as well as Indian and Pakistani nuclear forces) rehearse the "apocalypse" on a regular basis. It's not imaginary for them. It's their job description.

Missiles are fired from test sites, from missile silos, and from mobile launchers and submarines, a number of times a year by both the US and Russia. Most recently, these tests-cum-exercises have become increasingly public and threatening: Almost a form of political theater. It is a paradox of deterrence as routinely conceived—in my view a fatal paradox—that in order to maintain "strategic stability" we have to (incredibly but really) threaten the end of the world. In order to keep the end of the world off the agenda (i.e., frighten our potential adversaries into not doing anything we don't like) we have to keep the end of the world ON the agenda. But that means that the end of the world is indeed, ON the agenda … an absurd and fatal paradox. US and Russian exercises along the borders of the Baltic states should give rise to very deep concern.

There have already been too many "near misses". Deterrence depends on the impossibility of such mistakes. Statistically speaking we probably already shouldn't be here, and a study of those near misses leads one to conclude that the only reason we ARE here is by what General Lee Butler terms "Divine Providence". Without committing to any particular theology, we might well profitably ask, "just when does our miracle supply run out?"

Obvious "near miss" incidents include a number of sub–incidents during the Cuban Missile Crisis in one of which WW-III was nearly initiated by a wandering bear; incidents with computer tapes for "doomsday" in 1979, and with a malfunctioning computer chip in 1980 and 1981 (it happened three times). On the Russian side there was the famous incident involving Col. Stan Petrov of September 26,

1983; the Able Archer war scare just over a month later; and the Norwegian Weather Research Rocket incident of 1995, in which we are reputed to owe our existence to an unknown adviser who said "excuse me, Mr. President, let's wait another minute".

These incidents are described in greater detail in the Chatham House publication "Too Close for Comfort", launched in this very place, as well as in a number of my own panel presentations.

In recent years, greater attention has been given to the possibility of cyberspace attacks on nuclear command and control systems. The Vienna conference was addressed on that subject by Camille Francoise, and Jason Fritz addresses the problem in Hacking Nuclear Command and Control, written for the ICNND. The issue of cyberspace risks is addressed by a resolution adopted by the IPU, whose membership includes members of parliaments of both nuclear-armed states and those involved in "extended deterrence" relationships.

A number of things can be done to eliminate or reduce nuclear risk.

- First of all nuclear weapons can and should be eliminated yesterday. If nuclear weapons no longer exist then the risk of a catastrophic nuclear conflict, deliberate or inadvertent, can only be zero, at least in the short to medium term. This does not mean that all conflict will cease or that nirvana will instantly ensue. It merely means that lesser conflicts will no longer pose the risk of spiralling into an event sequence that risks human survival itself.

  Nuclear weapons are an existential threat to all humans including those not directly involved in any conflict. They must be treated as such and outlawed.

- Secondly, various stopgap risk reduction measures can be taken on the understanding that they are steps in a rapid movement to the complete elimination of nuclear weapons—steps that nonetheless may spell the difference between survival and extinction for humans.

These include:

- No longer targeting cities. Cities are not only the place where civilization "lives" in the most real sense, but if targeted they are in addition the source of the bulk of the 180 million tonnes of dark black smoke that will blot out the sun for decades after a large scale nuclear exchange.

- Taking nuclear weapons off high alert. I mentioned the six minutes of decision-making time which I've probably exceeded. This is an artifact of quick-launch, high-alert procedures that leave no time to ascertain whether or not an indication that the other has launched is really, really the end of the world approaching at three times the speed of sound, or merely a malfunctioning chip someplace. Much discussion has already taken place about increasing decision-making time, but lowering alert status is precisely about increasing decision-making time. Your attention is particularly drawn to the recent Op Ed in the NYT by Generals Vladimir Dvorkin and James Cartwright, former commanders of Russian and US missile forces, urging a lowering in operational status of nuclear forces. General Cartwright was here at the UN only yesterday.

- Establishing the Data Exchange Center that the US and Russian Governments have now agreed to set up three if not four times (first agreed in 1998 in the aftermath of the 1995 Norwegian research rocket incident), but which still has not been established.

- Moving the patrol areas of SLBMs further away from potential targets (Mosher Schwartz and Howell 2003). This would certainly increase warning times and make fingers on triggers less itchy.

- No First Use agreements/declarations.

Whatever we do—and some action is always better than none in this department though ALL of the above and more should be implemented as part of a quick path to zero—the catastrophic risk posed by nuclear weapons has always been nonzero, and has recently grown, probably by orders of magnitude.

Sooner or later the miracle supply really will run dry.

Unless we act.

Statement by People's Solidarity for Participatory Democracy

Speaker: Gayoon Baek

Madame President, delegates and friends of the NGOs,

This statement is a summary of joint declaration initiated by People's Solidarity for Participatory Democracy (PSPD) and Solidarity for Peace And Reunification of Korea (SPARK) and endorsed by around 300 individuals and 100 organizations around the world.

PSPD expresses its grave concerns on the ongoing armistice system on the Korean peninsula and urge relevant governments to end the Korean War to realize nuclear free Northeast Asia.

In the last 20 years, there have been several agreements to peacefully resolve the nuclear problems on the Korean peninsula, but no agreement has been fully implemented. As a result, the Democratic People's Republic of Korea (DPRK) has carried out nuclear tests on three different occasions. The nuclear crisis on the Korean peninsula has been aggravated because of accumulated distrust between the US and the DPRK, the DPRK and Republic of Korea (ROK) and neighboring countries and the DPRK. It is not the fault of only one country. All must accept responsibility.

In the last 20 years, unilateral US and its allies' policies against the DPRK, such as pressure and containment, the reinforced nuclear umbrella, have proved ineffective to resolve the DPRK nuclear issues. When dialogue and negotiations were pursued, the DPRK slowed or suspended its nuclear program. When hostile policies and sanctions were imposed, the DPRK developed it nuclear capabilities. In particular, the situation has become worse whenever the policy has been to halt dialogue, in the vain hope that regime collapse or transition was imminent.

In order to elicit a positive response from the DPRK, a new level of dialogue, bold, constructive proposals that are acceptable to both sides should be proposed. This new, comprehensive solution should be based on establishing a peace system on the Korean peninsula, normalizing relations between the DPRK and the US, and between the DPRK and Japan, and eliminating nuclear threats in Northeast Asia.

We propose as following:

- Immediately reconvene the lapsed Six-Party Talks based on the Joint Statement of September 19, 2005 in order to find ways to solve the nuclear crisis on the Korean peninsula.

- Parallel to, or proceeding, the Six-Party Talks, the countries involved—including South Korea, North Korea, the US, and China—should conduct negotiations that would lead to ending the armistice system and replacing it with a permanent peace system, based on the conclusion of a peace treaty.

- Parallel to, or proceeding, the Six-Party Talks, North Korea–US, and North Korea–Japan bilateral talks should be initiated in order to comprehensively improve relations between these states.

- The two Koreas should expand their dialogue and cooperation with each other, with the active support and encouragement of neighboring countries.

- There must be an end to the US–Japan–ROK military cooperation/alliance, including the missile defense system, which perpetuates the arms race on the peninsula and in the wider East Asian region.

- Japan must be prevented from exercising the right of collective self-defense, as interpreted by the Abe administration, because this would nullify the Japanese peace constitution, particularly article 9, which has served as an anchor of peace in East Asia.

- The denuclearization of the Korean peninsula should be approached based on perspectives on establishing a nuclear-weapon-free zone on the Korean peninsula or in Northeast Asia.

- Together with the conclusion of the Korean peninsula peace treaty, hostile military alliances must be phased out, stage by stage, and replaced by peaceful reciprocal relations, in order to contribute to the common security of the Korean peninsula and all East Asian countries.

I thank you, Madame President.

Statement by Setsuko Thurlow

Madame President, Distinguished Delegates, Ladies and Gentlemen,

On the cenotaph in the Peace Park in Hiroshima is an inscription that reads, "Rest in peace, the error will not be repeated." Instead of pointing an accusing finger at the United States the statement treats the issue reverently and philosophically as a crime against all of humanity. This has become the prayer and vow of many survivors who are determined to make sure that the deaths of their loved ones have not been in vain, and that no other human being will ever have to suffer the inhumane, immoral, cruel and indiscriminate effects of nuclear bombs.

Over the years, I have travelled the world to share my testimony as a Hiroshima survivor to help raise people's awareness of the danger of nuclear weapons. People's attitudes toward nuclear weapons have varied from indifference, justification and denial to fear and outrage. I find youth today more open and ready to learn the almost forgotten history of Hiroshima and Nagasaki. Never before in my work for nuclear disarmament have I felt such a sense of hopefulness and excitement as I do now.

Why do I feel so hopeful? It's because of the birth of a rapidly growing global movement with humanitarian initiatives in the recent years. This movement has been reframing the problem of nuclear weapons from deterrence credibility and techno-military issues to the issue of the humanitarian consequences. The result is a strong push for a nuclear Ban Treaty to achieve the prohibition and total elimination of nuclear weapons. Countries like Norway, Mexico and Austria, and international organizations such as the International Committee of the Red Cross and non-governmental organizations such as the International Campaign to Abolish Nuclear Weapons, and all of those who have collaborated to organize the three successful International Conferences on the Humanitarian Impact of Nuclear Weapons.

At the end of the Vienna Conference last December the Austrian Government unveiled the "Austrian Pledge" to fill the legal gap for the prohibition and elimination of nuclear weapons. They invited all NPT member states to support the Pledge so that meaningful discussion could take place at this Review Conference.

However, according to the news media, high-ranking officials of Norway and Japan admitted that the United States shamelessly approached them and pressured them to refrain from supporting the Austrian Pledge. Japan, a loyal ally and dependent of the US "nuclear umbrella", has not yet signed the Pledge. This kind of contradictory behavior of words and actions by the Japanese government has been deepening the distrust in the minds of Japanese people.

In international politics this kind of arm-twisting tactic or sabotaging behavior may be common among the Nuclear Weapon States and Nuclear Dependent States, but from the perspective of the majority of the people of the world such shady diplomacy is nothing but repugnant, and blasphemous to the lives of those incinerated by the bombing in Hiroshima and Nagasaki.

In 2009, in Prague, President Obama stated "As the only power to have used nuclear weapons, the United States has a moral responsibility to act" and he added "So today I state clearly and with conviction, America's commitment to seek the peace and security of a world without nuclear weapons." Several Japanese Prime Ministers have likewise publicly stated their support for nuclear disarmament. The often-repeated sentiment is that Japan, as the only nation that has suffered the atomic bombing, has a special responsibility to be at the forefront of the movement to abolish nuclear weapons. These leaders, of the nations that both introduced the nuclear age to the world and have the most intimate knowledge of the humanitarian harm that nuclear weapons cause, have described a role for themselves that they are currently negating.

Not only President Obama and Prime Minister Abe, but you, each and everyone of you NPT member delegates, agreed to Article 6 of this Treaty "to pursue negotiations in good faith on effective measures relating to cessation of the nuclear arms race at an early date and to nuclear disarmament." You are part of the decision making body for the fate of the human community and your responsibility is grave. Please break away from the non-productive past record on disarmament. After all, the NPT is 45 years old. The world is impatient.

As Foreign Minister of Sweden, Margot Wallström, has said, "If the current mechanism and forum continues to fail, we will need to consider other possible avenues for bringing disarmament work forward."

It is the 70th anniversary of the atomic bombings and the 70th anniversary of the United Nations. We need to reflect once again on the meaning of Hiroshima and Nagasaki and the meaning of the UN Charter "to save succeeding generations from the scourge of war."

On behalf of all the victims, from Hiroshima, Nagasaki, the Marshall Islands, French Polynesia, Chernobyl, Three Mile Island, US down-winders, Australian aboriginals, Kazakhstan, Fukushima and many others; and on behalf of all of us in the global community, I demand from the leaders of all nations: ban nuclear weapons, ban nuclear weapons now!

Thank you.

Statement by Sim Jin-tae

Recognize, Apologize, Investigate, and Compensate for A-bomb Damage Suffered by the Korean Victims!

My name is Sim Jin-tae, I am an Atomic Bomb survivor from South Korea.

I was born in Hiroshima in 1943. I was there when the atomic bomb dropped, and as a result, I became exposed to radiation.

At the time, 100,000 out of the total 740,000 victims were Koreans.

The majority of the Korean A-bomb victims were those who had been forcibly conscripted by colonial Japan.

My father too had been conscripted as a laborer at a military base in Hiroshima. 43,000 Korean survivors of the atomic bomb returned to South Korea after liberation.

But after living in abject poverty and facing social discrimination, many died from the aftereffects of the bomb without any medical care.

Currently, there are only 2,650 survivors registered in the South Korean Atomic Bomb Victims' Association.

But the Japanese government has ignored and discriminated the Korean A-bomb survivors. For decades, we each had to sue the Japanese government as individuals.

While the Japanese government covers the full cost of medical treatment for Japanese survivors, it discriminates against Korean survivors by limiting their medical coverage.

Japan needs to stop distorting the truth about its history of war and colonial conquest, and apologize to, as well as compensate the victims.

Despite predictions that the bombs would cause enormous damage, death, and injury, the United States chose to drop the first atomic bombs.

Therefore, the United States must take responsibility for its crime against the hundreds of thousands of A-bomb victims from 33 different nations, including Korea.

However, the U.S. has yet to even apologize for its crimes against humanity, let alone accept responsibility, even after 70 years.

The average age of the Korean atomic bomb victims is 81. Are they just waiting for all of us to die out?

An even greater problem is that radiation poisoning from the A-bombs is genetically transmitted to the following generations.

In 2013, South Gyeongsang Province in South Korea investigated 1,125 people, who were either first A-bomb victims or second or third generation descendants. 20.2% of descendants of survivors were found to have congenital deficiencies or hereditary diseases.

The 1,300 second-generation descendants who suffer transmittable diseases as a consequence of the A-bomb were and still are living proof that the humanitarian impact of nuclear weapons is permanent and is passed on through generations.

The U.S., Japanese, and South Korean governments must recognize the transmission of A-bomb damage to second and third generation descendants.

We demand an honest and sincere apology from the U.S. government before it's too late.

The South Korean government has also turned its back on the Korean A-bomb survivors.

We, the Korean atomic bomb survivors have come together with second and third generation descendants to lead a movement that will establish a special law for Korean atomic bomb survivors. At the very least, we want to build a memorial park for the Korean victims of the atomic bombs.

The South Korean government must exact from Japan compensation for A-bomb victims, a condition which was excluded from the treaty that normalized relations between Japan and South Korea.

Humankind must be made aware of the horrors suffered by A-bomb survivors in Korea and around the world. The United Nations, charged with guarding peace and human rights for all humankind, should take leadership and actively work to ban and eliminate all nuclear weapons.

Thank you.

Statement by Solidarity for Peace and Reunification of Korea
Speaker: Kim Hanna

The denuclearization of the Korean Peninsula

We express our greatest indignation against the incompetence and hypocrisy of the Obama administration, which undermines denuclearization of the Korean peninsula.

It is the incompetence of the Obama administration that is the greatest obstacle to denuclearization of the Korean peninsula.

The Obama administration's policy regarding North Korea is the so-called "strategic patience." It means that the United States will wait until North Korea abandons its nuclear capacity and insist that China persuade North Korea to give up its nuclear weapons. But this policy will only lead North Korea to strengthen its nuclear capacity.

It is the hypocrisy of the Obama administration that stands in the way of denuclearization of the Korean peninsula.

The Obama administration's so-called pivot to Asia and the construction of a missile defense system in Northeast Asia as well as the US–ROK–Japan alliance contain China and threaten preemptive strike against North Korea. As a result they create a structure of Cold War-like confrontation in Northeast Asia. To claim that it will achieve denuclearization of the Korean peninsula in such confrontation is pure hypocrisy.

Although North Korea declared its status as a nuclear weapons state in its constitution in April 2012, it has made clear multiple times since then its resolve for denuclearization of the Korean peninsula. But the United States has consistently ignored this.

On January 9, 2015, North Korea proposed that the United States "temporarily suspend joint military exercises in South Korea and its vicinity" in exchange for a temporary suspension of its nuclear tests. The United States turned down this proposal.

How can we expect a commitment to denuclearization of the Korean peninsula from the Obama administration when it turns down a proposal for the temporary suspension of nuclear tests even amidst widespread concerns about North Korea's impending 4th nuclear test?

The Obama administration seems interested only in securing North Korea's surrender through force and not in achieving denuclearization through dialogue. Why?

Isn't it true that the Obama administration has greater interest in expanding and reproducing confrontation and fanning an arms race in order to increase its arms exports to Northeast Asia? Isn't its aim to maintain its nuclear hegemony in Northeast Asia? Isn't its ulterior motive to use the structure of confrontation as justification for expanding NATO to the Asia Pacific region and merging it with the U.S.- Japan-Australia-South Korea alliance? And by doing so, isn't its aim to create a global military alliance and incapacitate the UN, thereby expanding its global military hegemony?

If not, then the United States should abandon its hypocrisy regarding denuclearization of the Korean peninsula and reverse course in its policy toward North Korea.

The days in which the United States has meddled with Northeast Asia—those days are past.

It should conclude a Peace Treaty on the Korean peninsula and move forward on establishing a peace regime. And as part of that process, denuclearization of the Korean peninsula can happen simultaneously.

There is no other path that is more meaningful for the realization of peace in the Asia Pacific region.

We urge all of you to also speak out against the Incompetence and Hypocrisy of the Obama Administration.

Statement by Terumi Tanaka

Speaker: Tanaka Terumi, Secretary General, Japan Confederation of A- and H-Bomb Sufferers Organizations (Nihon Hidankyo)

Hibakusha's Appeal

Hibakusha Reject Security Policies on Assumption of Possible Use of Nuclear Weapons: We Call on All States to Start Negotiations on Legally-binding Framework to Ban and Eliminate Nuclear Weapons

Chairperson, government representatives and NGO friends,

Thank you for giving me this opportunity to speak before you as an NGO representative.

The A-bomb attacks by the US on Hiroshima and Nagasaki on August 6 and 9, 1945 destroyed the two cities in an instant, killing more than 100,000 people immediately. A total of more than 200,000 lives were lost by the end of 1945.

The Hibakusha (the A-bomb survivors) continued to suffer from the after-effects of the bomb radiation, fear of death and various forms of discrimination. Up to date, several hundred thousand more people have perished from the A-bomb related causes.

I was caught by the atomic bomb in Nagasaki at age 13. I was upstairs in my house, located at 3.2 kilometers from the blast center. Suddenly I was engulfed in a brilliant flash. Frightened, I ran downstairs. As soon as I laid myself on the floor, I lost consciousness. After a while, hearing my mother calling me, I came to my senses and found myself under several panes of glass doors blown by the blast. I don't remember at all, but the blast might have blown through my house. Miraculously, the glass was not broken and I did not suffer any major injuries.

Three days later I entered the ground zero area, trying to find the whereabouts of my relatives, and was shocked at the terrible situation. I found one of my aunts and a cousin burned to death on the ground. Another aunt and my grandfather suffered heavy burns. Three days later, with my own hands I cremated the body of my aunt in the field. My grandfather who was in a critical condition followed her a few days later. My uncle, who had survived the bombing without external injuries and went away from the city to seek help, later developed a high fever and died after about 10 days. His body cells were destroyed by radiation.

The way they died was so painful and inhuman. Even three days after the bombing, within 2 kilometers radius of the blast center, many dead bodies were scattered unattended, and still more survivors with serious injuries and heavy burns were left without any relief.

Since that day, the souls of the surviving Hibakusha have continued to cry out, "Such atrocious crime should never have happened in human world, and must never be repeated."

However, under the 7-year occupation of the Allied Forces, the Hibakusha were prohibited from telling the truth. Were the occupation forces afraid that the inhumanity of the atomic bombing would be known to the world, or to the people of Japan?

The people's movement against nuclear weapons both in Japan and in the world, triggered by the damage of the hydrogen bomb test conducted at Bikini Atoll in 1954, encouraged the Hibakusha living across the country to stand up and get together, which led to the founding of Nihon Hidankyo, the organization of the Hibakusha in 1955.

For nearly 60 years since then, out of their own experiences the Hibakusha have continued to inform the public of the atrocious and inhuman nature of nuclear weapons both in Japan and internationally. Many Hibakusha travelled around the world to join demonstrations and mobilizations in the height of the global anti-nuclear movement in the late 1970s onwards. They appealed that the same suffering should never be repeated on anyone anywhere in the world, and nuclear weapons must be abolished even one day earlier.

Despite repeated crises in which nuclear weapons might be used, the human community has fortunately been spared of their actual use. A number of intellectuals have pointed out that the Hibakusha's appeals have contributed to preventing their use.

However, many Hibakusha leaders who worked in the frontline of the movement have already passed away without seeing the abolition of nuclear weapons. The average age of the surviving Hibakusha reached 80. Now the Hibakusha who were very young on that day are trying to inherit and speak the experiences of their parents and elder siblings, and their sufferings and hope for the future as Hibakusha.

In recent years, in the form of joint statements at the U.N. General Assembly and through the "International Conferences on the Humanitarian Impacts of Nuclear Weapons", an overwhelming majority of the countries in the world have agreed that "nuclear weapons must never be used under any circumstances." The appeals and stories of the Hibakusha are getting to have more and more weight in growing the international current for the abolition of nuclear weapons.

Now that nearly 70 years have passed, the Hibakusha cannot wait any longer. We refuse to accept any attempt to maintain and use nuclear weapons in the name of national security. We urge the nuclear weapon states and their allies to break away from their security policy based on "nuclear deterrence" and start negotiations on a legally binding framework to achieve the abolition of nuclear weapons.

Nuclear weapons are human invention. We can and must abolish them with human wisdom. Now is the time for us to mark a major step forward to abolish nuclear weapons without delay.

No More Hiroshimas! No More Nagasakis!

No More Hibakusha! No More War!

Statement by UNFOLD ZERO
Speaker: Aaron Tovish, Campaign Director, Mayors for Peace 2020 Vision Campaign

UNFOLD ZERO and Global Wave 2015

Your Excellencies, representatives of civil society, ladies and gentlemen,

UNFOLD ZERO is a platform that was established last year in order to highlight the role and possibilities of United Nations bodies and mechanisms to facilitate the achievement of a nuclear weapon free world.

The UN system has some flaws. Not all UN members subscribe to compulsory jurisdiction of the International Court of Justice. The P5 can block measures in the Security Council through their veto power. And any member of the Conference on Disarmament can block progress because of the tradition of requiring consensus. We concur with those who warn against repeating the mistake of relying solely on the CD to take forward multilateral nuclear disarmament negotiations.

On the positive side, the UN brings together all the key players relevant to the achievement of a nuclear weapons free world. This includes the nuclear-armed countries, the countries under extended nuclear deterrence relationships, the non-nuclear countries, and civil society actors engaged in nuclear disarmament.

The UN includes key organs through which nuclear disarmament agreements can be negotiated and their implementation monitored and enforced.

Importantly, the UN provides a cooperative security framework for addressing security challenges without recourse to the threat or use of nuclear weapons. This cooperative security framework provides possibilities to resolve these issues through diplomacy, negotiation, mediation, arbitration, adjudication, referral to regional authorities, and collective action to enforce peace and security based on the rule of law.

Unfold Zero aims to ensure that no possible avenue for achieving progress within the UN is left unexplored, not because everything must be done within the UN fold, but because if it can be done within the United Nations that is most often the best approach.

UNFOLD ZERO highlights some key UN initiatives for nuclear abolition, including:

- The proposal by Mexico to amend the Rome Statute for an International Criminal Court in order to include the use of nuclear weapons as a war crime under Article 8 para 2 (b) of the Statute;

- The UN Open Ended Working Group on Taking Forward Multilateral Nuclear Disarmament Negotiations. The OEWG sessions in 2013 were very productive in helping to outline the various options. Re-opening an OEWG process in 2016 could build on this to forge agreement on the most promising approach to commence negotiations.

- Elevating the issue with Heads of State and Government at the United Nations. Imagine the impact if every Head of State and Government representing a nation that has already renounced nuclear weapons stated emphatically at the UN General Assembly this September "Our security is enhanced from being a nation without nuclear weapons and we are proud of being part of the overwhelming majority of countries that have decided the same. We invite the nuclear reliant States to join us in reaping the even greater security benefits of a nuclear-weapon-free world."

- The High Level Conference on nuclear disarmament which the UN General Assembly has decided to convene no later than 2018. UNFOLD ZERO focuses on what might be a suitable preparatory process, what type of agreement could be adopted at this conference, and how to ensure participation by States at the highest level. Perhaps a revived OEWG could provide a suitable preparatory process.

- Cities are not Targets. Any attack on cities would constitute a violation of international humanitarian law, which prohibits use of weapons or military operations that target civilians or which cause indiscriminate harm to civilians. The Global Security Institute, a co-sponsor of UNFOLD ZERO, has proposed that the UN Security Council should affirm this—or if the Security Council fails to do so, the UN General Assembly should make such an affirmation.

A key aspect of UNFOLD ZERO is to educate civil society and policymakers about the possibilities for nuclear disarmament through the UN and through related mechanisms like the NPT.

The International Day for the Total Elimination of Nuclear Weapons, established by the UN in 2013, provides one platform for doing this. UNFOLD ZERO organised global actions including the UN Geneva commemoration in conjunction with the UN Office of Disarmament Affairs.

With regard to the 2015 NPT Review Conference, I wish to highlight Global Wave 2015—an action in which people all over the world "waved goodbye to nuclear weapons." The wave started with over 2000 people waving goodbye to nuclear weapons at the Peace and Planet rally in New York last Sunday.

It then swept around the world in 24 hours with over 100 exciting Global Wave actions in over 60 countries—nuclear armed and non-nuclear.

There were waves at schools & universities, homes & workplaces, city halls & parliaments, places of worship & interfaith gatherings, peace monuments & museums, at music festivals & sports events, on bikes and surfboards, at nuclear weapons deployment sites and production facilities, and at conferences and special anniversary events. Photos and videos of the wave actions are online, and a presentation of them will be made at a side event later in the NPT Review Conference.

Global Wave 2015 and UNFOLD ZERO join in calling on all governments to "wave goodbye to nuclear weapons" and establish a nuclear weapons free world.

Thank you.

Statement by the Western States Legal Foundation
Speaker: Andrew Lichterman, Senior Research Analyst

The Nuclear Danger Today: Existing Nuclear Arsenals are the Greatest Nuclear Threat

Good Afternoon. My name is Andrew Lichterman. This is the statement of the Western States Legal Foundation, based in California. The statement has been endorsed by over 100 organizations. This statement is titled The Nuclear Danger Today: Existing Nuclear Arsenals are the Greatest Nuclear Threat.

Five years ago at the 2010 Review Conference, the parties reaffirmed their commitment to a "diminishing role for nuclear weapons in security policies to minimize the risk that these weapons ever be used and to facilitate the process of their total elimination."[1] Since that time, there have been no initiatives from nuclear-armed states that hold promise to reduce nuclear arsenals below civilization-destroying numbers.[2] Instead, they are modernizing their arsenals to last far into the future. The *Bulletin of Atomic Scientists* Nuclear Notebook states that "[n]ew or improved nuclear weapon programs underway worldwide include at least 27 ballistic missiles, nine cruise missiles, eight naval vessels, five bombers, eight warheads, and eight

---

[1] 2000 Review Conference of the Parties to the Treaty on the Non-Proliferation of Nuclear Weapons, Final Document, Volume I, NPT/CONF.2000/28 (Parts I and II), p. 15; reaffirmed by 2010 Review Conference of the Parties to the Treaty on the Non-Proliferation of Nuclear Weapons, Final Document, Volume I, p. 19.

[2] "Not one nuclear weapon has actually been eliminated by a treaty commitment—we have witnessed instead only the voluntary retirement of certain obsolete weapons, with some caps on various deployments. And no nuclear disarmament negotiations have been underway in the 45-year history of the Nuclear Non-Proliferation Treaty, despite its obligation to undertake them." Angela Kane, United Nations High Representative for Disarmament Affairs, "The Nuclear Disarmament Regime?" EU Non-Proliferation and Disarmament Conference, Brussels, Belgium, 30 September 2013.

weapons factories."[3] To take just one example, the United States is planning to build 12 new ballistic missile submarines, each with 16 missile tubes that can launch multiple warhead missiles. They are expected to remain in service well into the second half of the 21st century.[4]

More alarming still, nuclear weapons have once more taken center stage in confrontations between the United States, its NATO allies, and Russia—countries that together possess most of the nuclear weapons that exist. They have turned a civil conflict in Ukraine into a violent proxy war in the borderlands of Europe. The tensions engendered by this confrontation have been intensified vastly—and potentially catastrophically—by the brandishing of nuclear arms by both sides. This has included forward deployments of strategic bombers to Europe by the United States, positioning of Russian strategic bombers in Crimea, and an accelerated tempo of military exercises and patrols both conventional and nuclear. And the confrontation in Europe is only one of several potential nuclear flashpoints, with new tensions and arms-racing from the Western Pacific to South Asia.

The possibility of an unintended incident spiraling out of control is real. But the greater danger is that the rulers of one nuclear-armed state will miscalculate the interests and fears of another, pushing some geopolitical gambit to the point where economic pressures, covert actions, low-level warfare and displays of high-tech force escalate into general war.

Those who rule in the nuclear-armed states have shown a shocking lack of judgment and foresight regarding what always has been the greatest danger: their own nuclear arsenals. Year after year, the five original nuclear weapons states issue joint statements congratulating themselves on their disarmament progress, which

---

[3] Hans M. Kristensen and Robert S. Norris, "Slowing nuclear weapon reductions and endless nuclear weapon modernizations: A challenge to the NPT," *Bulletin of the Atomic Scientists 2014*, Vol. 70(4) 94–107, 96.

[4] See generally Ronald O'Rourke, *Navy Ohio Replacement (SSBN[Xj] Ballistic Missile Submarine Program: Background and Issues for Congress*, Congressional Research Service, March 24, 2015.

they apparently see as more than adequate.[5] Only five years ago, in a statement issued just before the 2010 NPT Review, the President of the United States proclaimed that "[t]oday, the threat of global nuclear war has passed."[6] Less than two years ago, the U.S. Defense Department declared the most pressing nuclear dangers to be proliferation and "nuclear terrorism."[7] The time that has passed between those complacent statements and today's renewed nuclear confrontation is only the blink of an eye on the time-scale for disarmament contemplated by the nuclear-armed states.

Today's nuclear dilemma is clear. Without a profound change in the behavior of nuclear-armed governments, civilization-destroying arsenals will remain for many decades to come. The intertwined ecological, economic, and political crises of the 21st century are hurtling ahead at the pace of a modernity dependent on exponential growth heedless of nature's limits. This now is generating tensions that raise the danger of war among nuclear-armed countries on a time-scale measured in months and years, not decades and decades.

National security technocrats talk of "managing" the rise of new powers. But a social order rapidly approaching its limits will generate conflict in ways both expected and unpredictable—and likely unmanageable. Most unmanageable of all is the discontent generated by a global economy that serves only a fraction of the population, leaving hundreds of millions of people utterly desperate and billions more with little hope for a better future. Those who rule the most powerful countries seem determined to repeat the mistakes of the past, manipulating the resulting rage and despair to set us against each

---

[5] See, e.g., "Joint Statement from the Nuclear-Weapon States at the London P5 Conference," U.S. Department of State, Office of the Spokesperson, February 6, 2015; "Joint Statement on the P5 Beijing Conference: Enhancing Strategic Confidence and Working Together to Implement the Nuclear Non-Proliferation Review Outcomes," U.S. Department of State, Office of the Spokesperson, April 15, 2014; "Fourth P5 Conference: On the Way to the 2015 NPT Review Conference," U.S. Department of State, Office of the Spokesperson, April 19, 2013.

[6] The White House, Office of the Press Secretary, Statement by President Obama on the 40th Anniversary of the Nuclear Nonproliferation Treaty, March 05, 2010.

[7] U.S. Department of Defense, *Report on Nuclear Employment Strategy of the United States Specified in Section 491 of JO U.S.C.*, June 12, 2013, p. 2.

other in their struggles for wealth and power without end. Nuclear weapons are the ultimate expression of the irrationality of this order of things, and may also be the instrument that ends it, destroying all of our futures.

It may seem impossible to address all of these crises at once, but we have no choice. Our survival depends on transforming mutually reinforcing patterns of injustice and distrust, self-sustaining cycles of violence, and unsustainable ways of living into their opposite. Our common future rests on our willingness to trust that committed, urgent efforts to build a fair and democratically controlled economy, develop sustainable technologies, and to disarm and disassemble the military-industrial complexes of the 20th century will build upon and reinforce each other. Those at the apex of the global war system must start taking apart the apparatus of annihilation that has distorted human development immeasurably for generations. It is up to all of us to take apart the machinery of injustice and oppression, and to build a new economy and society in balance with the ecological rhythms of our planet. It is long past time. Let us begin.

Statement by the World Council of Churches
Speaker: Emily Welty

Faith Communities Concerned about the Humanitarian Consequences of Nuclear Weapons

Since August 1945, when the cities of Hiroshima and Nagasaki were subjected to atomic attack, the continued existence of nuclear weapons has forced humankind to live in the shadow of apocalyptic destruction. Their use would not only destroy the past fruits of human civilization, it would disfigure the present and consign future generations to a grim fate.

Nuclear weapons are incompatible with the values upheld by our respective faith traditions—the right of people to live in security and dignity; the commands of conscience and justice; the duty to protect the vulnerable and to exercise the stewardship that will safeguard the planet for future generations. Nuclear weapons manifest a total disregard for all these values and commitments. There is no countervailing imperative—whether of national security, stability in international power relations, or the difficulty of overcoming political inertia—that justifies their continued existence, much less their use.

We raise our voices in the name of sanity and the shared values of humanity. We reject the immorality of holding whole populations hostage, threatened with a cruel and miserable death. We urge the world's political leaders to muster the courage needed to break the deepening spirals of mistrust that undermine the viability of human societies and threaten our shared future.

For decades, the obligation and responsibility of all states to eliminate these weapons of mass destruction has been embodied in Article VI of the Treaty on the Non-Proliferation of Nuclear Weapons (NPT). Progress toward the fulfillment of this repeatedly affirmed commitment has been too slow; today it is almost imperceptible.

Instead, ongoing modernization programs divert vast resources from limited government budgets when public finances are hard-pressed to meet the needs of human security. This situation is unacceptable and cannot be permitted to continue.

Therefore as people of faith, we pledge to:

1.   Communicate within our respective faith communities the inhumane and immoral nature of nuclear weapons and the unacceptable risks they pose, working within and among our respective faith traditions to raise awareness of the moral imperative to abolish nuclear weapons;

2.   Continue to support international efforts to ban nuclear weapons on humanitarian grounds and call for the early commencement of negotiations by states on a new legal instrument to prohibit nuclear weapons in a forum open to all states and blockable by none.

As people of faith, we call on the world's governments to:

3.   Heed the voices of the world's *hibakusha* (atomic bomb survivors) urging the abolition of nuclear weapons, whose suffering must never be visited on any other individual, family or society;

4.   Take to heart the realities clarified by successive international conferences on the humanitarian impact of nuclear weapons; take concrete action leading to the complete elimination of nuclear weapons, consistent with existing obligations under the NPT.

5.   Associate themselves with the Pledge delivered by Austria at the Vienna Conference and pursue effective measures to fill the legal gap for the prohibition and elimination of nuclear weapons.

Statement by the Women's International League for Peace and Freedom

Speaker: Mia Gandenberger

Thank you, Chair.

This morning states began their work on nuclear disarmament in Main Committee I. We are looking forward to an intensive debate about how to achieve the full objectives of article VI in this body. As an NGO that monitors implementation of NPT agreements, we have to say that there is much work to be done in this area.

Five years after the adoption of the NPT Action Plan in 2010 it is clear that compliance with commitments related to nuclear disarmament lags far behind those related to non-proliferation or the so-called peaceful uses of nuclear energy.

On nuclear non-proliferation, states were mainly asked to "stay the course," hence, there has been success in implementing the actions in the area of nonproliferation.

A positive development since the adoption of the 2010 Action Plan has been the negotiations between Iran and the E3/EU+3, which led to the agreement of a Joint Plan of Action. The parties are still engaged in negotiations to reach a comprehensive agreement.

With regard to the actions on the "peaceful uses" of nuclear weapons, the most serious development since the adoption of the action plan has been the Fukushima nuclear disaster, which put the issue of nuclear safety at the centre of this section of the action plan. Other work on this issue has been ticking along, though we agree with those NPT state parties that have rejected nuclear power as part of their energy mix due its negative implications for health, environment, safety, and disarmament.

But while the NPT states parties are getting along with the implementation of these aspects of the Treaty, of the 22 actions related to disarmament, only five have seen concrete progress.

Yet during the same five years, new evidence and international discussions have emphasized the catastrophic consequences of the use of nuclear weapons and the unacceptable risks of such use, either by design or accident. The NPT's full implementation is as urgent as ever, but 70 years after the use of nuclear weapons in Hiroshima and Nagasaki and 45 years after the NPT's entry into force, the promise of disarmament remains unfulfilled.

The five NPT nuclear-armed states have not met their limited commitments, which did not even require direct action to fulfill article VI's obligation of multilateral negotiations to end the nuclear arms race and eliminate nuclear weapons and delivery systems.

It is true there have been reductions of nuclear arsenals since the Cold War. But most of these reductions occurred before the 2010 Review Conference. And they have been countered by modernisation programmes, through which the nuclear-armed states have invested billions of dollars to extend the lives of and "upgrade" their remaining arsenals.

On their own, reductions are not disarmament. Reductions do not take away the risk of use, intentional or accidental. Reductions do not fulfill article VI's obligations for multilateral negotiations for nuclear disarmament and cessation of the nuclear arms race. And reductions are ineffective if nuclear-armed states continue to modernise and improve their nuclear weapons and delivery systems, extending the lives of these systems for perpetuity.

Non-nuclear-armed states, on the other hand, have initiated and led new meetings and processes related to nuclear disarmament, such as the conferences on the humanitarian impact of nuclear weapons, the open-ended working group on nuclear disarmament, and the high-level meeting on nuclear disarmament.

As a result, the discourse around nuclear weapons is changing. Even in the NPT context, nuclear weapons are now being viewed and described as dangerous and unacceptable weapons.

The 2010 NPT Review Conference expressed "deep concern at the catastrophic humanitarian consequences of any use of nuclear weapons." Since then, these consequences have increasingly become a focal point for discussion and proposed action.

Rather than being divisive, the humanitarian initiative has provided the basis for a new momentum on nuclear disarmament. It has involved new types of actors, such as the Red Cross and Red Crescent Movement, the United Nations Office for Coordination of Humanitarian Affairs, the United Nations Development Programme, and a new generation of civil society campaigners.

The discussion around the humanitarian impact of nuclear weapons has grown into the most positive development around nuclear weapons in many years, and should be fully supported by all states parties to the NPT.

It has also resulted in the Austrian Pledge, which commits its government (and any countries that wish to associate themselves with the Pledge) to "fill the legal gap for the prohibition and elimination of nuclear weapons." Today, 78 states have endorsed this Pledge.

These states are committed to change.

These states believe that existing international law is inadequate for achieving nuclear disarmament and that a process of change that involves stigmatizing, prohibiting, and eliminating nuclear weapons is necessary.

Yet some states here seem to insist on maintaining the status quo. This is a time for progress, not procrastination.

In the coming weeks, states parties will have to undertake a serious assessment of the last five years. They will also have to determine what actions are necessary to ensure continued survival of the NPT and to achieve all of its goals and objectives, including those on stopping the nuclear arms race, ceasing the manufacture of nuclear weapons, preventing the use of nuclear weapons, and eliminating existing arsenals.

Will another agreement on steps or building blocks lead to that?

We think no. We think it is time for those states committed to nuclear disarmament—the majority of countries—to take action now to start a process to prohibit nuclear weapons, even if the nuclear-armed states or some are not yet ready. It's time to start seriously fulfilling the objectives of the NPT.

www.ingramcontent.com/pod-product-compliance
Lightning Source LLC
Chambersburg PA
CBHW052105270326
41931CB00012B/2892